Ca ʌ ,

C000002132

Michael Morpurgo

Author Study Activities for Key Stage 2

Sally Wilkinson

David Fulton Publishers
London

David Fulton Publishers Ltd
The Chiswick Centre, 414 Chiswick High Road, London W4 5TF

www.fultonpublishers.co.uk

First published in Great Britain in 2003 by David Fulton Publishers

Copyright © Sally Wilkinson 2003

British Library Cataloguing in Publication Data
A catalogue record for this book is available from the British Library.

ISBN 1-85346-927-0

The materials in this publication may be photocopied only for use in the purchasing organisation. Otherwise, all rights are reserved. No part of this publication may be reproduced, stored in a retrieval system or transmitted, in any form, or by any means, electronic, mechanical, photocopying, recording or otherwise, without the prior permission of the publishers.

Author Study Series
Series editors: Eve Bearne and Helen Bromley

Also available in this series:

David McKee: Author Study Activities for Key Stage 1
by Sally Elding (ISBN 1-85346-934-3)

E. Nesbit: Author Study Activities for Key Stage 2
by Helen Bromley (ISBN 1-85346-933-5)

Cover design and poster design by Martin Cater
Designed and typeset by Kenneth Burnley, Wirral, Cheshire
Printed and bound in Great Britain by Thanet Press Limited, Margate, Kent.

Contents

Acknowledgements   iv

Introduction   v

Map of contents   vii

1 Biographical information   1
- Biographical activities   6

2 Narrative structure and storyline   15
- Activity: Creating a temperature chart   17
- Activity: Structuring a story   18
- Activity: Story webs   21

3 Characters   23
- Activity: Creating a character sketch   26
- Activity: Writing in role   29

4 Settings   33
- Activity: Analysing setting   35
- Activity: Focus on illustrations   38

5 Themes   39
- Activity: Book boxes   41

6 Comparing stories – teaching sequence over five lessons   43

7 In close: teaching sequence   49

Acknowledgements

I would like to thank Helen Appleton from Tudor Primary School, Sudbury, Suffolk and Diane Shah from Acton Primary School, Suffolk for trialling some of the materials, and also the children in their classes for their excellent work, examples of which are included in this publication.

Thanks also go to Clive and Bryn for their patience and support.

The publishers would like to thank Christian Birmingham (through his agent, Alan Manham), and Egmont Books for their permission to use the artwork and book covers which appear on the pull-out poster. Cover illustrations from *Kensuke's Kingdom* and *War Horse* © 2000 Michael Foreman; *Escape from Shangri-La* and *Why the Whales Came* © 1999 Claire Fletcher.

Introduction

This author study resource book is organised so that you can choose to focus on one or more aspects relating to the author Michael Morpurgo. The plan below gives an outline of how the materials in the book could be used over four weeks.

Author study plan

Days	Focus
1–5	• Introduce Michael Morpurgo. • Read biographical extracts in shared reading. • Interview the author (teacher in role). • Alter and add to the biographical extracts in shared writing to include information that the children have found out. • Write biographical information for a book cover. • Write an article about the author.
6–15	• Focus on one story with the whole class in shared reading and writing. • Use drama techniques to bring the story to life. • Write in role and in response to the drama work. • Use other single texts and themed book boxes for group work.
16–20	• Compare the characters, setting and plot in stories by Morpurgo that the children know well. • List similarities and differences between two books. • Create a mind-map linking books to each other by character, setting or plot. • Summarise single books through freeze-frames and story webs.

There are suggestions for whole class work and group work. Some activities have been noted as suitable for a focus group – the group which the teacher works with during the course of the session. Throughout the material links are made with the National Curriculum and the Literacy Strategy Framework.

National Literacy Strategy references to this type of work

Biographical Objectives

Y2: T3 Read information about authors.

Y3: T3 Be aware of authors.

Y4: T1 Find out more about popular authors.

Use this information to move on to more books by favourite authors.

Y5: T1 Consider how texts can be rooted in the writer's experience.

Author study Objectives

Y2: T3 Compare books by the same author, evaluate and give reasons for preferences.

Y3: T3 Compare and contrast works by the same author.

Y4: T3 Read further stories by a favourite writer, making comparisons and identifying familiar features of the writer's work.

Y6: T3 Compare and contrast the work of a single writer.

Map of contents

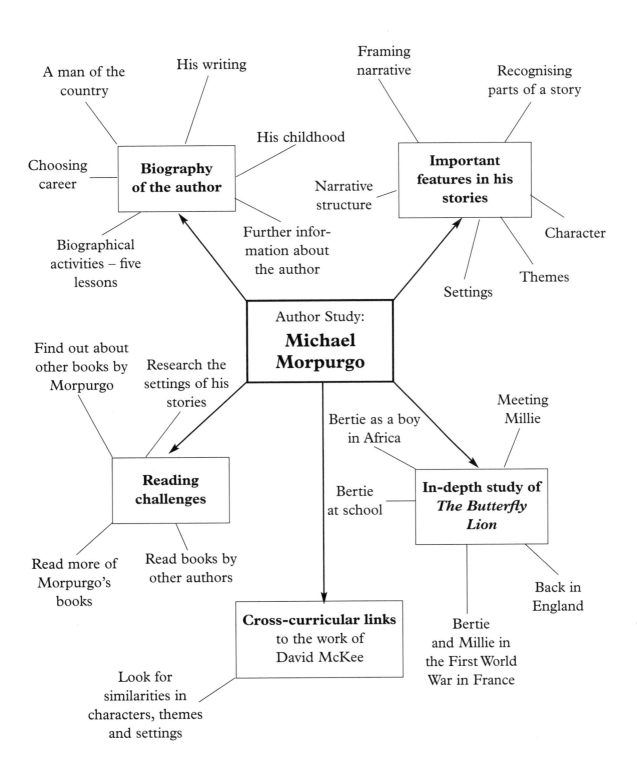

1 Biographical information

Michael Morpurgo is an author who is worth getting to know well. The more you find out about his life and interests, the more you see how these are echoed in his books. He would not say that he writes books; he writes stories that are *about* children – not *for* children. First, they have to fascinate him, or he would not be able to write them, both him as an adult and the child within him. He says that 'researching a book is *me* being a child. I want to know'. He hopes that his stories help children open their eyes against complacency and prejudice.

A man of the country

Michael Morpurgo was born in 1943. He has now written over 60 books and many of these draw on his passion for the countryside, animals and farming. His interest in farming also led to him and his wife, Clare, founding the charity 'Farms for City Children'. They now run three farms in Devon, Pembrokeshire and most recently in Gloucestershire. *Sam's Duck* is dedicated to one of them, Nethercott, where the story is also set. The farms give 3,000 children a year who live in urban areas the chance to stay on a farm and contribute to its daily life by helping with jobs like feeding the animals, tending the crops and mucking out stables. Iddesleigh, the village in Devon where Nethercott Farm is situated, appears in several of Michael's books. Nethercott Farm is the setting in *Farm Boy* and *War Horse*, with both books being dedicated to the people of the village.

Michael Morpurgo's favourite holiday haunts also appear in his stories. He and his family have spent many happy times on the Scilly Isles, which are now the setting for three of his books. Here they enjoy walking and sailing. One of his sons is a keen birdwatcher, and *Why the Whales Came* originated while on holiday with him on the Scilly Isles. The idea for the deserted island of Samson that is at the heart of the story came from a true local tale. Another favourite haunt is the island of Bryher, the setting for *The Wreck of the Zanzibar*. The name of the ship came from a family story that his mother loved to tell. Apparently when Michael was three she found him rocking on his bed, chanting 'Zanzibar, Marzipan, Zanzibar' over and over for no particular reason.

His childhood

Michael Morpurgo draws on other childhood memories in his stories. As a child he lived in London, except for a short period during the war when the family was evacuated to the countryside. After London they moved to Bradwell-on-Sea in Essex, a setting which features in *Escape from Shangri-La* as the childhood home of Cessie's dad. From here he went to boarding school, first a prep. school in Sussex and then King's School in Canterbury. At the former he often suffered from homesickness, like Albert in *Butterfly Lion,* and he didn't feel that he was very academically minded. He didn't enjoy English lessons, particularly writing, and although there were some authors whom he would read avidly, he wasn't a bookworm – this came later on. Once at Canterbury he found his niche as an important member of the school rugby and cricket teams and developed his love of music.

Choosing a career

After a brief spell training in the army at Sandhurst, Michael Morpurgo realised that army life was not for him. He married Clare and after completing a degree in English Literature became a teacher, first of secondary age children and then in a primary school. The children he taught were the first to hear his work. At this time these were mostly short stories and Michael realised that he could do something powerful with the written word as he captured his children's attention with the stories that he had written. After eight years of teaching both Michael and Clare wanted to continue working with children, but to do so in a different context that would enable them to have more of an impact on children's lives and change their perceptions of the world. Through a family inheritance they were able to set up the first of their 'Farms for City Children' at Nethercott. This special farm, where children from towns and cities can be the farmers, has provided first-hand experience of the countryside and the opportunity to work together. From here on, Morpurgo combined writing with working on the farm.

His writing

One crucial aspect of the writing process that Michael Morpurgo emphasises is that it is important to dream. This way, he says, the story grows inside you over time. He mulls over ideas for plots, characters and settings in his head when he's working on the farm or even on holiday. Most of the major books he's written have taken him about a year. Only when he feels the story is ready will he write it down. His favourite place to write is on his bed, often with his dog beside him. He doesn't like to redraft his work, so he tries to get it right first time, filling the pages with as much writing as possible so that he doesn't have to begin a blank page (another thing he dislikes doing). He has many more ideas than ever make it into print and finds that sometimes working on one idea can lead to an even better one that he wasn't expecting. Once the book is written, Morpurgo likes to share his dream with the children who are staying on the farm. His wife also reads all his first drafts as he values her opinions.

Other aspects of Michael Morpurgo's life that are reflected in his stories come from incidents that have happened to him or that he has witnessed, and influences in his own life. He did not get to know his father until he was in his twenties as his parents separated when he was very young. He had a good relationship with his stepfather and was also very attached to his grandparents. There is a very good account of how he and his brother came to meet their father in the autobiographical short story 'My Father is a Polar Bear' in the collection *Hereabout Hill*. The title of the story comes from a picture Michael had as a child of his father playing the character of a polar bear in a play. He and his brother actually got to see him acting in it, but it was not until many years later that he met him when he returned to England from his home in Canada to act in another play.

The theme of relationships between the old and the young has been one which Michael has explored in many of his books, and that comes from his experiences as a child, but also more recently as a grandfather himself. He captures well the close bond of trust and understanding that can exist between the old and the young. (See 'Relationships with grandparents and older people', p. 37.)

Michael Morpurgo has carried out extensive research for many of his books. His interest in the First World War appears in several stories and was developed through detailed detective work involving long hours reading, visiting the Imperial War Museum and also through talking to men from Iddesleigh who experienced it first hand in the trenches. Their recollections have enabled Michael to give stories like *War Horse* depth and sincerity. Research and his own experiences have also fuelled his interest in the Second World War. He draws on memories from his own childhood, as growing up just after the war in London he remembers the bombed-out ruins, the rationing, the smog and what adults talked about at that time.

One subject Michael Morpurgo was good at at school was French. This ability has stayed with him and now he is often asked by French schools to come to talk to their pupils. Several of his grandchildren are also bilingual. Morpurgo would like to see more books in translation so that children have the opportunity to read about how others live throughout the world. Many of his own books have been translated into over twelve languages. Morpurgo worries that the dominance of the English language means that children in the United Kingdom have fewer opportunities than any other country in Europe to read books by foreign writers. This, he feels, narrows our view of the world and risks us becoming arrogant and isolated as a nation. In children's bookshops on the European mainland you will find books in a variety of languages. This enables children to read about a wider range of people and places, seeing differences and similarities and empathising with others. Morpurgo sees the visits he makes to schools in the Netherlands and France as important for him and the children he talks to. They get to know more about him and the United Kingdom through him, and he gains understanding of them.

Michael Morpurgo has done much for children's literature, not just through his own work, but also through the co-founding (with Ted Hughes) of the Children's Laureate. This position has been created to celebrate writers and illustrators of books for children. Morpurgo believes strongly that children deserve adults to write well for them. He is still attached to authors and books that were special to him as a child. When he was presented with the Children's Book Award for *Kensuke's Kingdom* he said of this story:

Two of my favourite books are *Treasure Island* and *Robinson Crusoe*, so it is no accident that I have written books about islands – *The Wreck of the Zanzibar* and *Why the Whales Came*. But I have always yearned to write my own desert island story.

Further sources of biographical information

- 'My Father is a Polar Bear'. A short story in *Hereabout Hill* where Morpurgo narrates how he came to meet and get to know his father.
- Article in *Books for Keeps No. 79*, March 1993. Your Schools Library Service may keep back copies of this magazine or it may be possible to obtain information from Peters Library Service address.
- Interview with Michael Morpurgo for *Young Writer* magazine, Issue 12. A large part of the interview is available on their website at www.mystworld.com/youngwriter.
- A good biographical piece and information about some of his books is available on Channel 4's education website at www.4learning.co.uk/bookbox/authors/morpurgo.
- Author profile direct from the publisher HarperCollins or from Books for Students booksellers.
- *An Interview with Michael Morpurgo* by Joanna Carey is one of the *Telling Tales* series published by Mammoth.

Michael Morpurgo

Biography Extract 1

Michael lives with his wife Clare in the village of Iddesleigh in Devon. Their home is close to Nethercott Farm, one of three 'Farms for City Children' that they run.

Michael spends a lot of his time working with the children who visit the farm. About 3,000 children stay for a week on one of their farms every year. The children care for the animals, collect the eggs from the hens, muck out stables and look after the crops.

When he is writing, Michael likes to sit on his bed. He thinks about his stories for a long time before he starts writing. When he has finished a book he often shares it with the children who are staying at the farm.

Michael Morpurgo

Biography Extract 2

Michael Morpurgo was born in 1943. He is married and has three children (two sons and a daughter) and four granddaughters.

Animals and children are important to Michael. He works with them both on Nethercott Farm. This is the setting for *Sam's Duck* and several more of his stories. He uses another of his favourite places, the Scilly Isles, as the setting for *The Wreck of the Zanzibar*.

When he was at school Michael did not like writing. He thought that he was not very good at school work. When he left school he joined the army, but soon after he realised that this wasn't what he wanted to do. He went to college and became a teacher. He started writing short stories for the children in his class. They liked them so much that he decided to become a writer.

Michael has now written over 60 books. He likes writing about the countryside, animals and children having adventures.

Biographical activities

Objectives
- To create biographical blurb.
- To make a magazine page/webpage article about Michael Morpurgo.

Starting off with biographical information is a good way of introducing a writer to the children. Hopefully some of them will have heard of the author and read one or two of his books. During the first lesson you will be able to gauge who are already fans of his work so that in future lessons they can take a lead in recommending further titles to the rest of the class. These children may also be able to move more quickly on to activities involving comparison of two or more of Michael Morpurgo's books. (See activities Comparing Stories.)

Resources
Any of the following books link with Michael Morpurgo's biography:

'Farms for City Children' charity Nethercott Farm	*Sam's Duck* *Farm Boy* *War Horse* *Sam's Duck* *Mossop's Last Chance* and others in the Jets series about Mudpuddle Farm
His school life	*Butterfly Lion*
How he met his father	'My Father is a Polar Bear' in *Hereabout Hill*
Scilly Isles where he spends holidays used as settings	*The Wreck of the Zanzibar* *Why the Whales Came*
Childhood home of Bradwell-on-Sea	*Escape From Shangri-La*
Knowledge of sailing	*Kensuke's Kingdom*

Teaching sequence
This is an outline for a series of lessons based on biographical information and a selection of Michael Morpurgo's books that are suitable for the class. The biographical extracts are enlarged and used as the shared text. For a more detailed extract for group work use part of the teacher's notes (e.g. his childhood and career) or one of the other sources of biographical information mentioned on page 4.

Days	Whole class work	Group work
1.	• Oral book review • Shared reading biography extract • Ask questions	1. Read 'blurbs' 2. Categorise questions 3. Reading with teacher
2.	• Shared reading biography extract 2 • Ask and answer questions	1. Read biographical information 2. Read with teacher 3. Prepare questions
3.	• Shared writing biographical piece for a book cover	All write a short biographical piece for a book cover using a word processor if possible. Teacher with focus group.
4.	• Teacher in role as Morpurgo • Plan article on Morpurgo	All plan a magazine or web page article on Morpurgo. Teacher with focus group.
5.	• Shared writing article on the author	All write a magazine or web page article on Michael Morpurgo. Teacher with focus group.

Lesson 1

Whole class work

Begin by giving an enthusiastic and brief review of a book by Michael Morpurgo that you have read. This could be one that you are intending to use with the class, so don't give everything away, just enough to whet their appetites!

Introduce the author to the children through shared reading of biography extract 1 (p. 5).

Ask the children what else they would like to know about the author and make a list of their questions, using a separate piece of paper or card for each one.

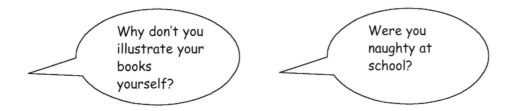

Why don't you illustrate your books yourself?

Were you naughty at school?

Group work

Read the 'blurb' (for independent learners)
You could put a piece of tape or an elastic band round the books to make sure the group read no further.

- In pairs, read the 'blurb' on the back covers of several of Michael Morpurgo's books.
- You are going to report back to the rest of the group and/or the class about one book you would like to read, and why.
- How does the 'blurb' entice you to read the book?
- Do you like the sound of the plot, the characters or the setting of the story?
- Make sure you can explain *why* you want to read the book, not just say 'It looks good.'

Categorise biographical questions (mixed ability group)

- Group the biographical questions collected by the class, e.g. childhood, his books, his family.
- If you have time, add extra questions.
- Display the questions and add information added as you find out details about his life.

> When did you first start writing?

Focus group
With the group read the first chapter of one of Michael Morpurgo's stories. Can they see any links with his life?

Lesson 2

Whole class work
Shared reading of biography extract 2 (p. 5). The dedication in the front of *Sam's Duck* goes well with this as it gives extra information about the 'Farms for City Children' charity. Ask the children if this extract provides the answers to any of the questions they asked in Lesson 1. Write the answers alongside the displayed questions.

Group work

Find out more about Michael Morpurgo (independent learners)
The further biographical information could be part of the biography on pages 1 to 4 or from the other sources given on page 4.

- Read the information you have got about Michael Morpurgo.
- Underline or circle any information that is new to you.
- Does this new information answer any of the questions that the class has asked about Michael Morpurgo? If so, add it to the display of questions.
- Share any new information you have found with the rest of the class.

Ask questions about Michael Morpurgo (children who need support)

> • What would you like to know about Michael Morpurgo and his books? Use the sentence starters below to help you write your questions.
>
> Do you . . . ? How do you . . . ?
>
> Why did . . . ? If you could . . . ?
>
> What is . . . ?

Tell the children that in a lesson this week they will have an opportunity to ask Michael Morpurgo more questions about his life, as you will be taking on the role of the author.

Focus group

With the group read the first chapter of one of Morpurgo's stories. Can they see any links with his life? (See grid linking aspects of his life with book titles on p. 6.)

Lesson 3

Whole class work

Show the children an example of a piece of biographical information on the cover or inside the dust jacket of a novel. Explain that none of Michael Morpurgo's books have this and ask them what they think would be the most important pieces of information to include in a short biographical piece.

Through shared writing show the children how you use the two biographical extracts to create information for a book cover. Either using a word processor or, with scissors and paper, demonstrate selecting, ordering and adding information to create the new text. Involve the children in suggesting the next sentence or how to combine two pieces of information.

Group work

Creating a biographical 'blurb'

The children could work individually or in pairs (using a word processing program if possible). The 'blurbs' could then be photocopied and fixed inside the books themselves to give information to other readers.

> • You are going to write a short piece of biographical information for the inside cover of one of Michael Murpurgo's stories.
> • Use the facts that your teacher has read with you or you have found out for yourself.
> • Decide on three or four things about Michael that will interest the reader.
> • Decide on the best order to give the reader the information.
> • Try out different ways of giving the information. Which sounds the best?

King Arthur

Michael Morpurgo

Michael Morpurgo was born in 1943. He went to boarding school when he was seven. His favourite sports were Rugby and Cricket. His favourite lesson was french.

When he left boarding school he joined the army, but then he found out that he didn't want to be in the army all his life. So he went to university and became a teacher, and it was then when he started to be a writer.

He went on holiday and fell in love with a girl called Carla. When he got home he married Clare. They had three baby's. two sons and one daughter. He has four granddaughters that are bilingual, he is bilingual to.

He and his wife setup the charity Farms for City Children. Michael has three farms.

Michael gets the ideas for his books by looking in newspapers, asking the children that stay at his farm and daydreaming with his dog. Some of his books are The Dancing Bear Sams Duck, The Butterfly Lion and Jiggers day off. His favourite books are Treasure Island and wing in the willos. Michael is Sixtynine now

Biographical blurb from Tudor Primary

Focus group
Discuss the selection and ordering of information with the group. Try out some sentences orally and on whiteboards if available. Ask the children to add words or re-order sentences to improve the information they are giving the reader.

Lesson 4

Whole class work
For this lesson you could put yourself in role as Michael Morpurgo or enlarge some of the biographical information from pages 1 to 4 to provide the answers to the children's questions. There may be questions that you are unable to answer, so the children need to be aware that it will not be possible to find out everything that they want to know. Begin with the children who were in Group 3 in Lesson 2 asking their prepared questions and then encourage others to join in.

Orally and in diagrammatic form plan the headings for an article on Michael Morpurgo and demonstrate how to list the main aspects under one heading using bullet points.

Group work

Planning an article about Michael Morpurgo (for children needing support)
The children could work in pairs or threes making notes under the headings. These could then be copied for the children to use individually in Lesson 5.

Use the headings below to help you plan your article about Michael Morpurgo:

- Introduction
- When he was young
- His books
- Conclusion

Focus group
With the children choose the information for each heading and decide how to record this in note form.

Use the headings below to help you plan your article about Michael Morpurgo:

Introduction

When he was young

His books

Conclusion

Lesson 5

Whole class work
Show the children the layout of an article or interview with an author. (See the sources at the end of the biography section.) Basing your writing on this model, write the start of an article for a magazine or web page about Michael Morpurgo's life and work based on the plan from Lesson 4. This could be under specific headings or in a simple question and answer format as if interviewing the author.

Group work
Individually the children write an article based on their plan from Lesson 4.

Focus group
Discuss with the children the order of information under one of the headings and the structure of individual sentences. Ask the children to rehearse their sentences orally and/or record a sentence on a whiteboard so that they can improve it.

Important features in Michael Morpurgo's stories

Once you start reading one book by Michael Morpurgo you find yourself looking for the next. He is a writer who draws you into his stories, involves you with his characters and makes you laugh and cry. He has written books for an extensive audience on a wide range of subjects across many settings, often involving his characters in adventures and unravelling mysteries. He is a consummate storyteller. His distinctive style allows a story to unfold so that none of the detail is missed and yet the urge to know what happens next keeps you turning the pages. Whilst Morpurgo doesn't allow the reader to dawdle, he does enable you to experience his characters' emotions.

Many of his stories are written in the first person, allowing some of the main characters to talk directly to the reader and share their innermost thoughts. The children, who are the main characters in his books, are easy for the reader to identify and empathise with. Many are loners, some by choice and some because of their situation. There is plenty of action, but he also allows his characters to reflect on what they see, hear and believe. Through the characters that he creates he explores (and enables his readers to explore) issues of responsibility, freedom and self-esteem.

Reading one of his well-known stories can lead you to others with similar settings, themes or characters. Many of the significant themes that recur in Morpurgo's books have direct links to his own life.

The following sections have activities linked to them that enable children to explore the narrative structure, main characters, themes and settings of his stories.

Narrative structure and storyline

- Recognising parts of a story.
- Framing narrative.

Characters

- Children who are solitary or isolated.
- Children who are bullies.
- Not liking school.

Settings

- Farm and country life.
- A desire to see the world.

Themes

- Caring for animals.
- Relationships with grandparents and older people.

2 Narrative structure and storyline

Background

Michael Morpurgo's stories have a strong narrative drive that give them pace and keep the reader hooked. To help the children see how Morpurgo has structured his stories it helps to divide them up into their main parts. There are various terms used for describing these. Below, the sections are referred to as opening, climax, development, resolution and ending. The development is used to describe the main body of the story and can contain further climaxes, developments and even 'mini' resolutions that sort out some minor parts of the story, leaving the main final event for the resolution itself.

In some of his books Michael Morpurgo uses the technique of a framing narrative that introduces and concludes the story. This structure is very similar to a common one used in folk tales, called a frame story. In both *The Wreck of the Zanzibar* and *Butterfly Lion* this allows the reader to travel back in time. Interestingly, the narrator in both of these stories is also called Michael.

In *The Wreck of the Zanzibar* the framing narrative introduces the island of Bryher to which Michael has travelled for the funeral of his great aunt Laura. This leads into the main story which is told through diary entries that Laura made when she was fourteen. At the conclusion of the diary entries the story returns to the present day. The framing narrative ends with an important symbol of the story, the figurehead from a boat in the shape of a turtle, being given to the children of Bryher. In *The Butterfly Lion*, the framing narrative is also in the present. The story of young Michael and Millie in old age is framing the main story, but Michael finds echoes of his own life in that of Bertie, Millie's husband. (See p. 45 for an in-depth study of this book.)

NLS reference to this type of work

The National Curriculum for English makes specific reference to developing awareness about narrative both in the reading and writing requirements for Key Stages 1 and 2. The National Literacy Strategy promotes the use of texts to identify text structures that can be replicated, to plan in 'markers about the direction of the story' and to 'borrow from the narrative style of quality writers' (DfEE, NLS Flier 6). Teachers are directed to help their pupils to look for patterns and common features (DfEE, NLS Flier 3), investigate through reading, sequence, compare basic story elements such as beginnings and endings, pick out significant incidents, identify and discuss reasons for events in stories linked to plot, and in writing to plan in advance, use writing frames, use their knowledge of story elements.

Specific NLS references

Y2:T2   To predict story endings/incidents.

Y3:T2   To plan main points as a structure for story writing.

Y4:T1   To explore narrative order.

Y5:T3   To identify the point of view from which a story is told.

Y6:T1   To manipulate narrative perspective.

Activities

- Creating a temperature chart.
- Structuring a story.
- Story webs.

Activity: Creating a temperature chart

Objective
- To explore narrative patterns in Michael Morpurgo's stories.
- To recognise key parts of the story.

Resources
Copies of *The Dancing Bear, Tom's Sausage Lion* and *Butterfly Lion*. Other books could also be used for these activities.

Whole class work
Many of Michael Morpurgo's stories have a straight chronological pattern that can be represented diagrammatically. Below is a temperature chart showing the main events in *The Dancing Bear* created in a shared writing session that shows the highs and lows of the story very clearly. The dotted centre line represents when the story could be said to be at a point of equilibrium. Main events are then plotted above and below the line according to whether they are a high point (a time of happiness or excitement) or a low point (a time of sadness, fear or when things are going badly for the main characters). Examples of other stories that could be represented in this way are *Why the Whales Came, Conker,* and *Tom's Sausage Lion*.

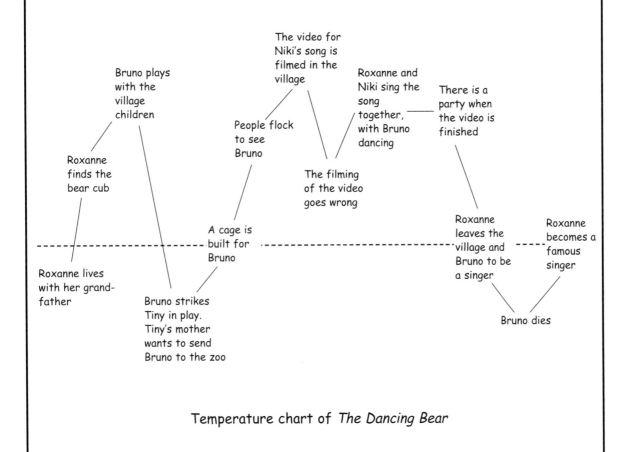

Temperature chart of *The Dancing Bear*

Activity: Structuring a story

Objective
• To recognise key parts of the story.

Resources
Copies of *Tom's Sausage Lion.*

Other books could also be used for this activity.

Photocopiable sheets of **Sections of the story** (p. 20).

Whole class work
On completion of one of Michael Morpurgo's books, discuss where each section of the narrative begins, using the following headings:

Opening This may include details of characters, and time and place of the setting.
Climax This is when the action begins and the plot takes off.
Development This is when the action becomes more involved. There are often further climaxes, developments and even resolutions to parts of the story.
Resolution A final event sorts everything out and you can sense the ending coming.
Ending Things are brought to a satisfying conclusion and the theme of the story is often returned to.

The example below was created in a shared writing session following the reading of the book by a group in the class. It could be used as a whole class activity to identify sections of the story. If you wanted to create a plan for *The Wreck of the Zanzibar* or *The Butterfly Lion* you would need to include two extra headings at the beginning and end for the opening and ending of the framing narrative (see above).

Group work
Using the example, groups could identify the sections of another story such as *The Dancing Bear, When the Whales Came* or *Kensuke's Kingdom*, which have similar structures.

Further suggestion
Groups could be asked to represent the parts of the story in pictures. Prior to doing their drawings, discuss the different sections and create a freeze-frame for each one so that the children are very clear about the moment in the story that they will draw. It works well to start with an image from the main body of the story (the development) as this is often the hardest part for children to identify and work backwards to the climax and the opening. Then return to the development and work forwards to the resolution and ending. When all five freeze-frames have been decided on, ask the children to do them in the order they appear in the story.

Sections of the story

Title: Tom's Sausage Lion

Opening

On Christmas Eve Tom sees a lion eating sausages.
He tells his mum, dad, aunt and uncle, but no one believes him.

Climax

On Christmas Day Tom sees the lion again — eating scraps of turkey out of the dustbin. When everyone else looks the lion has gone and Tom's dog Sam is eating the scraps instead.

Development

Tom looks for the lion. He tells everyone at school about it, but no one believes him. Then Claire says she's seen the lion too.
Tom's father finds some sheep have been killed and blames Sam. However, Tom realises Sam tried to protect the sheep from the lion. Tom meets the lion and finds out he is tame.

Resolution

Tom takes the lion to Claire's and then together they parade the lion to school and to the police station.

Ending

The lion's owners collect him. Tom's mum and dad apologise for not believing him.

Sections of the story

Title:

Opening

Climax

Development

Resolution

Ending

Activity: Story webs

Objective
* To focus on time sequences.
* To recognise the features of a frame story.

Resources
Copies of *The Butterfly Lion*.
Other books could also be used for this activity.

Whole class work
Several of Michael Morpurgo's novels involve characters looking back in time. This is an important part of the stories which involve relationships between children and older people. The story web of *The Butterfly Lion* on p. 22 shows how the main narrative about Albert, Millie and the lion is contained within the framing narrative about the young Michael running away from school.

As a way of helping the children recognise the way a story is framed, as a class activity, begin to create the frame and the main story. The children could then use this to complete the story web for themselves or to create story webs from other Morpurgo stories they know.

Any of the episodes notes on the web could be used for a range of other activities, such as hot-seating characters (see Chapter 3), to delve below the surface of the storyline.

Once the children are familiar with making story webs they can use them to plan their own narrative sequences.

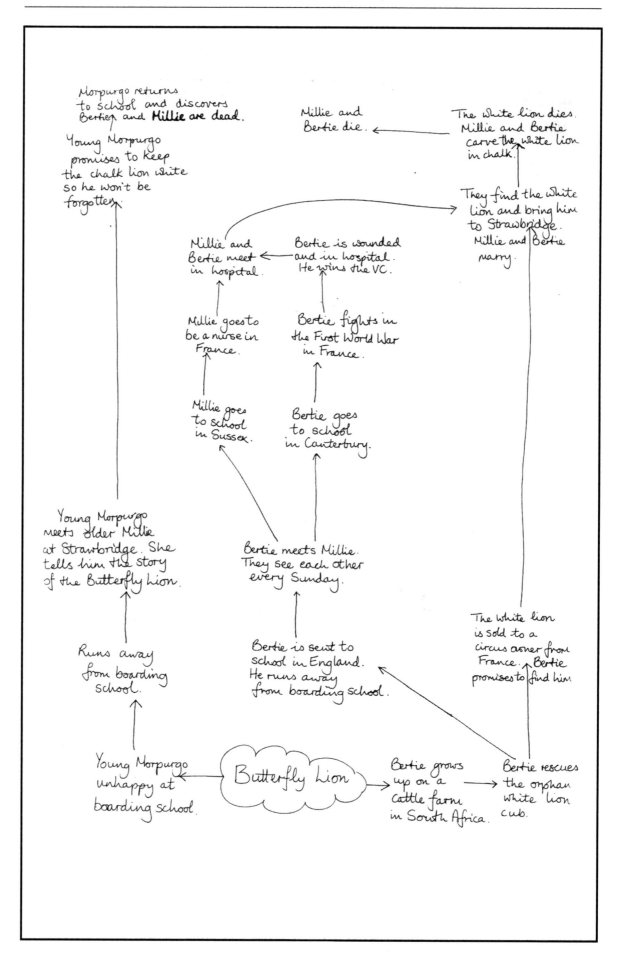

3   Characters

Background

Michael Morpurgo has both boys and girls as the main characters in his books. Most of the characters have these traits in common:

- A goal towards which they are working and will not be shaken from.
- A strong sense of what is right.
- Self-reliance.
- A love of animals.
- An ability to empathise with others (mostly animals or older adults).

The girls that Morpurgo portrays often have to overcome stereotyping of their gender by others. Laura in *Wreck of the Zanzibar* and Gracie in *Why the Whales Came* both fight to be given the same chances as boys. Laura wins her battle when she takes her brother's place in the gig that rescues the sailors from the Zanzibar when it hits rocks off the coast of Bryher.

Children who are solitary or isolated

Michael Morpurgo often stresses that the children who are isolated or solitary in his stories are not actually lonely:

> She was a solitary girl, but never lonely, I think. At school she appeared to be a dreamer, a thinker. (Roxanne, in *Dancing Bear*, p. 10)

> Bertie had no friends to play with, but he always said he was never lonely as a child. At night he loved reading his books and losing himself in stories, and by day his heart was out in the veld with the animals. That was where he yearned to be. (Bertie, in *Butterfly Lion*, p. 25)

These children show an inner strength and depth of character. They use their imaginations and have dreams that they believe will come true. They are self-reliant and seek out their own destiny.

Even when the children do have friends these are not always important to the story. In *Kensuke's Kingdom* Michael's best friend Eddie moves house near the beginning of the story (Chapter 1) and this provides a clue that things are going to change for him and his mum and dad.

Michael Morpurgo also uses the school holidays as a time period in which to isolate the main character from their peers. In *Escape from Shangri-La*, when Cessie returns to school after the holidays she tries to keep the others from school in the dark about her grandad. At first Tom, in *Tom's Sausage Lion*, thinks that it will be good to share his sighting of a lion with everyone when he returns to school after Christmas. He soon regrets it, though, as he is teased by his peers and accused of lying by his teachers (Chapter 2, p. 20). However, one good thing does come from it as he gets to know Clare, a quiet girl he had not paid attention to before. She has also seen the lion and provides the meat from her dad's butchery business that helps to capture him.

Children who are bullies

Quite a few of the main characters in Michael Morpurgo's stories have to overcome bullies. Sometimes this takes the form of intimidation, with the protagonist disbelieving and putting the main character down. In *Why the Whales Came* Daniel's brother Big Tim refuses to believe what his younger brother tells him about the birdman and shows how harmful ignorance and gossip can be (Chapter 9, p. 103). This also happens to Cessie in *Escape from Shangri-La* when Shirley Watson spreads malicious gossip about her grandad (Chapter 1, p. 13). At first, Cessie's reaction is to avoid Shirley and her gang, but the climax comes when the gang in the park taunts her grandfather. This gives Cessie the strength to confront Shirley at school and overcome the fear she has of her. Likewise Tom, in *Tom's Sausage Lion*, is teased and cowered by Barry Parsons (Chapter 2, p. 18). However, at the end of the story it is Barry who is intimidated as Tom leads Leo the lion into the school playground to prove to everyone that he was not imagining it or lying when he said that he had seen a lion (Chapter 6, p. 66).

Nick's Grandma in *Conker* gives him sound advice on dealing with bullies when she helps him overcome Stevie Rooster:

'Didn't you tell me once that he likes to call himself the "Conker King of Jubilee Park"?'
'Yes.'
'Well then,' said Grandma. 'You've got to knock him off his throne, haven't you?'
'But how?'
'You've got to beat him at conkers.' (p. 14)

Children and teachers

This is another area that has close links with Michael Morpurgo's own life. He was sent away to boarding school and was at times very unhappy there. In *Butterfly Lion* he uses these experiences to provide the background to the story of Albert and the lion. At the start of the book the young boy, who we later find out is Morpurgo himself, runs away from the school, as Albert had done years before. He shelters in the big house with the lion on the gateway where Millie tells him the story. The reader is only let in on the fact that the young boy is the author when he asks a teacher about Albert near the end of the story.

I looked up at the honours boards around the dining hall, at the names of all the
boys who had won scholarships over the years. I looked for Bertie Andrews. He

wasn't there. But then, I thought, why should he be? Maybe, like me, he wasn't brilliant at his school work. Not everyone wins scholarships:

Cookie – Mr. Cook, my history teacher – was sitting beside me at the end of my table. 'Who were you looking for, Morpurgo?' he asked suddenly. (From *Butterfly Lion,* p. 121)

The notion of not being very good at school work and of school being a chore that has to be got through is evident in several stories. In *Why the Whales Came* Gracie and Daniel each have different skills and support each other in school, but neither is keen to go and they 'bunk off' as often as possible (Chapter 3, p. 36). Schools and teachers are often portrayed as places and people that do not help the children overcome their troubles or support them. However, there are exceptions, as in *Dancing Bear* where the schoolteacher narrates the story. He acts as Roxanne's confidant, and while he stops short of advising her, he does help her with her grandfather and to look after Bruno. In *Farm Boy* school knowledge is also given credit as the grandson completes his engineering degree before returning to the farm to work with his grandfather. In this story the grandson also becomes his grandfather's teacher as he helps him overcome his inability to read and write (p. 44). This is another fascinating glimpse of events from Michael Morpurgo's own life. His own grandfather also shared the secret of his illiteracy with him when he was a young boy.

NLS reference to this type of work

The National Curriculum for English and the National Literacy Objectives contain references to the study of book characters, their actions, how a character copes with problems and challenges and how the character changes and develops with the plot line:

To develop their understanding . . . pupils should be taught to identify and describe characters, events and settings in fiction (3a). (NC KS1 for Reading)

To develop understanding and appreciation of literary texts pupils should be taught to identify how character and setting are created (4c). (NC KS2 for Reading)

Specific NLS Objectives

Y2:T2   To write character profiles.
Y3:T2   To identify and discuss main and recurring characters; to write portraits of characters.
Y3:T3   To discuss characters' feelings and behaviour.
Y4:T3   To identify social, moral or cultural issues in stories, e.g. the dilemmas faced by characters.
Y5:T1   To investigate how characters are presented.
Y5:T3   To write from another character's point of view.
Y6:T1   To plan quickly and effectively the plot, characters and structure of their own narrative writing.

Activities

• Creating a character sketch.
• Writing in role.

Activity: Creating a character sketch

Objective
- To understand the complexity of characters and their feelings.

Resources
Copies of *The Wreck of the Zanzibar.*

Enlarged photocopiable **Character Sketch** sheet (p. 28).

Whole class work
A teacher drew up the following character sketch of Laura with her class during a shared writing session following the reading of Chapter 1 of *The Wreck of the Zanzibar.* This could be added to after reading further chapters, either by the whole class or as a group activity.

Further suggestions
The **Character Sketch** sheet can be used for any character in any of Michael Morpurgo's novels. Pupils could be asked to use the sheet to write about the character from different points of view. You could select characters in the novel who might have different views about the person who is the focus of the sketch and ask pupils to compile a range of different opinions of the character involved. This can then form the basis of group discussion which depends on evidence from the novel to support particular views.

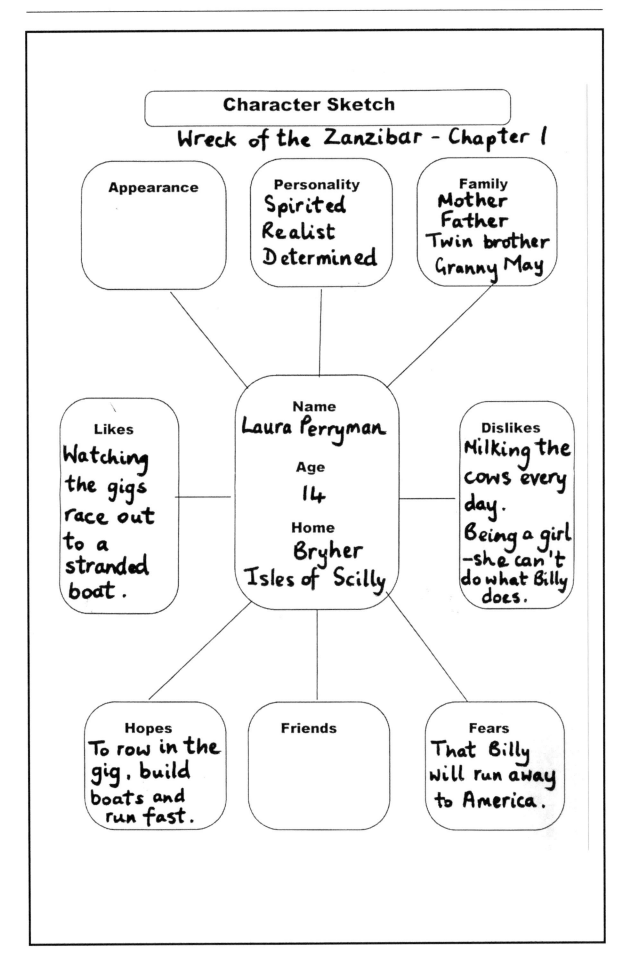

Character Sketch

Wreck of the Zanzibar - Chapter 1

Appearance

Personality
Spirited
Realist
Determined

Family
Mother
Father
Twin brother
Granny May

Likes
Watching
the gigs
race out
to a
stranded
boat.

Name
Laura Perryman

Age
14

Home
Bryher
Isles of Scilly

Dislikes
Milking the
cows every
day.
Being a girl
—she can't
do what Billy
does.

Hopes
To row in the
gig, build
boats and
run fast.

Friends

Fears
That Billy
will run away
to America.

Character sketch

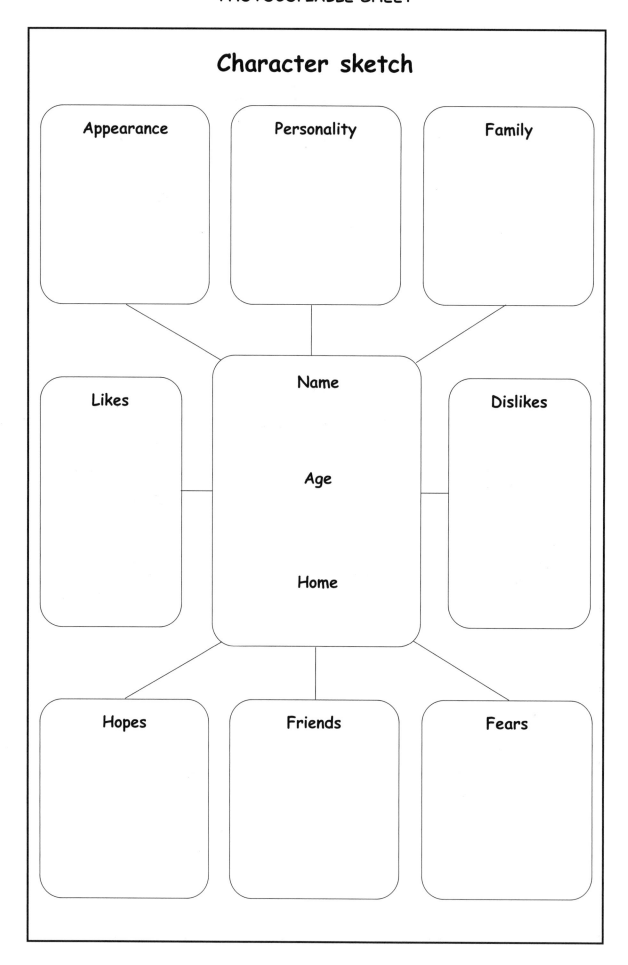

Appearance

Personality

Family

Likes

Name

Age

Home

Dislikes

Hopes

Friends

Fears

Activity: Writing in role

Objectives
- To look at the story from a particular viewpoint.
- To understand something about motivation and emotions as depicted in the stories.
- To write in role.

Resources
Copies of any of: *The Wreck of the Zanzibar, Butterfly Lion* or *Escape From Shangri-La.*

Enlarged copy of Roxane's letter and copies for group work.

Enlarged copy of Tom's diary entry and copies for group work.

Whole class work followed by individual or group work
Decide whether you want the children to write a diary entry or a letter to another character. In shared reading look at a model of the appropriate format. *The Wreck of the Zanzibar* provides a good model for diary entries as the main story is written in this format. There are also letters to use as models in *Butterfly Lion* (Collins 1996, p. 76) when Albert writes to Millie and in *Escape From Shangri-La* when Cessie writes to her mum and dad. (Mammoth 1998, p. 143).

Following discussion of the format in shared reading, develop a letter or diary entry in shared writing that the children will then respond to in role. The example of a letter comes from shared writing completed when the class had read *The Dancing Bear.* The teacher and children composed the letter from the school-teacher to Roxanne and then the children replied as if they were Roxanne or Niki. The diary entry was also completed in shared writing during the reading of *Tom's Sausage Lion.* The children could write following entries based on later events in the story.

The School House
Gimmelwald

Dear Roxanne,

It has been very quiet in the village since you left. All the singing and dancing that we did seems like it was a dream.

I often hear you and Niki singing on the radio and the other day, when I was sitting with Monsieur D'Arblay in the café, I saw you on the television. Your singing was, as always, angelic.

I'm afraid I have some very sad news for you. Soon after you left the village Bruno died. He was not ill and did not suffer. One minute he was sitting up in his cage waiting for his food and the next he was dead. I know this will upset you, but be brave and remember all the good times you had together.

If you have any spare time in between all your recording and performing the whole village would love to see you.

Best wishes

Your Bear Sitter

January 7th

I thought today was bad enough with all the trouble I got into at school, but when I got home things got even worse. At school nobody would believe me about the lion. Barry kept teasing me until I just couldn't take any more – he deserved that punch! The only person who believed me was Clare. We have worked out a plan to tempt the lion with some meat and then take its photo, but I can't wait until tomorrow – not with what has happened to Sam today.

Dad has decided that he killed some of our lambs. I know it was the lion, but of course Dad didn't believe me – so I ran out to find Sam. When I eventually found him he had a gash on his leg, but I couldn't bring him home or Dad would have had him put to sleep so I washed his leg and laid him in Ghost Cottage. Tomorrow Clare and I will prove that lion exists.

4   Settings

Background

Farm and country life

Michael Morpurgo sets many of his stories in the countryside and on farms. He uses the village of Iddesleigh (where he lives) in *War Horse* and *Farm Boy* and sets *Why the Whales Came* and *The Wreck of the Zanzibar* on the Scilly Isles where he has had many holidays. He also involves boats and sailing, another of his pastimes, into many of his stories. In *Why the Whales Came* Gracie and Daniel love making and sailing model boats (Chapter 1) and in *Kensuke's Kingdom* Michael and his mum and dad set off to sail around the world (end of Chapter 1, p. 15).

Michael Morpurgo feels strongly that children should have an understanding of country and farm life, as can be seen from his dedication in the front of *Sam's Duck*. In his stories he is never guilty of romanticising rural life. In *Tom's Sausage Lion* the lion kills three lambs and Tom's dad, believing the killer to be Tom's dog Sam, threatens to shoot him, as he can't afford to lose valuable lambs (Chapter 3, p. 33). The value of the animals is emphasised again in *The Wreck of the Zanzibar* when first one of the cows dies in childbirth (p. 26) and then the others perish when a gigantic storm hits the island. Animals are never kept for their own sake; they always have a role to play. In *War Horse* Albert has to train Joey to pull the plough or his father says he will get rid of him. While the children might become attached to the animals on the farm, the reader is never allowed to forget that they are there for a purpose. The children themselves also have their part to play on the farm. They are expected to carry out particular duties. This is what Billy dislikes in *The Wreck of the Zanzibar* and so he runs away to sea to escape the daily grind of farm life, and milking the cows in particular.

A desire to see the world

Billy chooses the life of a sailor as his way of seeing the world, but for Roxanne it is the glamorous life of a pop singer that entices her away. In *Dancing Bear* a contrast is set up between the people making the pop video and the quiet village community that they have come to use as their set. Both Billy and Roxanne are entranced by a character who comes from outside their own community; someone who is different, interesting and talks of exciting people and places. For Billy, Joseph Hannibal's tales of exotic places are just too hard to resist and although the man himself turns out to be a scoundrel, meeting him still launches Billy on his trip across the seas. However, like the grandson in *Farm Boy*, who travels to Australia, goes to college and then returns to his grandfather's farm; Billy does return. Roxanne, though, never returns and it is left to the teacher to tell the reader that he still hears Niki, the pop star she left the village with, and Roxanne singing on the radio, so we presume that the glamorous life is still suiting her.

When Michael's father is made redundant in *Kensuke's Kingdom* he persuades his wife and Michael that they should use the redundancy money to sail around the world. The doubt and uncertainty of being unemployed is replaced by that of the open ocean. In contrast to the characters who want to see the world, in *Butterfly Lion* Albert's mother cannot stand the wildness and vast spaces of the African savannah and talks to Albert of the rural landscape back in England that was her home and to which she dreams of returning.

NC/NLS reference to this type of work

In the National Curriculum for Key Stage 1 pupils should be taught to:

3a: identify and describe characters, events and settings in fiction;
3b: use their knowledge of sequence and story language when they are retelling stories and predicting events.

At Key Stage 2 in order to develop understanding and appreciation of literary texts, pupils should be taught to:

4c: identify how character and setting are created.

The National Literacy Strategy has specific references to work on setting and time/sequence. These require pupils to be able to talk about the setting of a story using pictures, words and phrases; to think about how different settings are built up from small details and how they influence events; the sequencing of events and an understanding of time and sequential relationships, i.e. what happened when, and to compare and contrast stories with a variety of settings.

Specific NLS objectives

Y3: T1 To develop the use of settings in own stories.
Y3: T3 To plot a sequence of episodes modelled on known story.
Y4: T2 To compare and contrast settings across a range of stories; to develop the use of setting in own stories.
Y4: T2 To understand how the use of expressive and descriptive language can create mood.
Y6: T1 To prepare a short section of a story as a script, using location/setting.

Activities

- Analysing setting.
- Focus on illustrations.

Activity: Analysing setting

Objective
- To focus on an extract to analyse the setting of the story.

Resources
An enlarged copy of a short piece of text from a story that the children have been reading that contains a good description of the setting. Individual copies of another extract describing a setting from a known book by Morpurgo.

Copies of the photocopiable sheet **Analysing setting** (p. 37).

You may want to use an enlarged copy of the completed example provided.

Whole class or guided group work
Place the enlarged extract in the centre of a flip-chart or a large sheet of paper and around it note the answers to the questions in the framework example:

- Which words or phrases are important to the description of the setting? Are any similes or metaphor used?
- Choose three words that describe how a character in the story feels about the setting.
- Decide on three words that describe how you feel about the setting.
- What words or phrases can you suggest would add to the description of the setting?
- What other books by Michael Morpurgo have a similar setting?

List words and phrases either from the text or from the children's response to it.

The following example is from a Year 6 class studying *Kensuke's Kingdom*. A blank of this framework is on page 37.

Questions for Analysing Setting

List the words or phrases that are important to the description of the setting. Are any similes or metaphors used?

Shaped like an elongated peanut
long swathe of brilliant white beach
Slopes steeper and more thickly
wooded twin peaks.
green jewl of an island sea –
and silken shimmering blue

exotic .
isolated
beautyful

Write three words that describe how you feel about the setting.

Robinson
Cursoe .

Lord of the flies .

The turtle and the Island .

The island looked perhaps two or three miles in length, no more. It was shaped like an elongated peanut, but longer at one end than the other. There was a long swathe of brilliant white beach on both sides of the island, and at the far end another hill, the slopes steeper and more thickly wooded, but not so high as mine. With the exception of these twin peaks the entire island seemed to be covered with forest....I remember thinking how wonderful it was, a green jewel of an island framed in white, the sea all about it a silken shimmering blue. Strangely, perhaps comforted somehow by the extraordinary beauty of the place, I was not at all down-hearted. One the contrary I felt strangely elated. I was alive.

Kensuke's Kingdom p53

Write three words that describe how a character in the story feels about the setting.

wonderful
beautyful
elated .

Beach like sifted flour .
twin peaks ~ that cut through
the blanket of the forest .

List the titles of any other stories that have a similar setting.

Write words, phrases or a sentence that will add to the description of the setting.

PHOTOCOPIABLE SHEET: Analysing setting

List the words or phrases that are important to the description of the setting. Are any similes or metaphors used?

Write three words that describe how you feel about the setting.

Write three words that describe how a character in the story feels about the setting.

Place text extract here.

List the titles of any other stories that have a similar setting.

Write words, phrases or a sentence that will add to the description of the setting.

Activity: Focus on illustrations

Objectives
- To understand how illustrations add to a sense of setting and how atmosphere is created.
- To understand how expressive and descriptive language can create mood and atmosphere

Resources
Any of Michael Morpurgo's picture books, such as *Sam's Duck, Silver Swan* or *Wombat Goes Walkabout,* all of which are illustrated by Christian Birmingham.

Alternatively, one of his illustrated novels, such as *The Wreck of the Zanzibar* (illustrated by Christian Birmingham) or *Farm Boy* (illustrated by Michael Foreman).

Guided group or whole class work
Look at one or more illustrations and read the text that accompanies the part of the story that is being illustrated. Make a list of the aspects that the illustration has added to the knowledge and understanding of the setting.

This could be:

- the colours used;
- the style of drawing/painting; for example, are the outlines sharp or shaded?
- the detail of parts of the setting;
- whether the image is close-up or long distance.

Ask the children to decide on an illustration that they would like to have been present in one of the books they have read. They then describe the illustration and say how it would have added to the book in terms of deepening understanding, knowledge or appreciation of the story. You could do this first with the whole class, modelling how you would write such a description and then offer it as an independent or focus group activity.

The children's illustrations can be part of the reading area or an 'author focus' display.

Further suggestion
Choose an evocative illustration and model how to describe it in words. This makes a good activity for developing writing to create atmosphere.

5   Themes

Background

Caring for animals

Michael Morpurgo often involves the children in his stories in saving animals from cruelty or death. He believes that there is a strong connection between children and animals, which enables them to understand each other:

> Animals bring out a strong sense of fairness, of what's right in young children. I see this all the time.

In the picture book *Sam's Duck*, Sam is staying on Nethercott Farm with his class from school (one of Morpurgo's 'Farms for City Children'). Sam visits the local animal market and buys a white duck to save it from being eaten. With the help of the elderly gardener he keeps it a secret and when he returns home makes a present of it to his grandad. Another important aspect of this theme then comes into play as grandad helps Sam realise that a flat is not a good home for a duck. They let him go on the pond in the park so that he can be with other ducks and be free.

Michael Morpurgo writes about lions in two stories. Tom's experience of lions in *Tom's Sausage Lion* is very different from Bertie's in *Butterfly Lion* (see page 45). On Christmas Day he's sure that he can see a lion rifling the bins for turkey scraps outside the window, but when he calls his family to look all they see is his dog, Sam. Everyone teases Tom about seeing the lion and even accuses him of lying. Events take a more serious turn when Sam is accused of killing three of Tom's dad's sheep. Tom knows that it must be the lion and, aided by his friend Clare, sets out to clear Sam's name. When Tom tracks the lion down he finds that it's tame and that it has an owner. He and Clare set out to return Leo to his owner and on the way teach all the people – particularly the adults who wouldn't believe that the lion existed – a lesson as they march Leo first to school and then through the town to the police station.

Often significant older adults are involved in helping the children rescue animals. In *Conker* Nick is helped by his grandma to save an alsatian who is being badly treated. After discovering the animal Nick goes home to think up a plan to rescue him. When he returns to offer the dog's owner his most treasured possession, his bike, in return for the dog, he is distraught to find that it has gone. However, his grandma has saved the day as she has realised what Nick was trying to do and with the local vet already persuaded the cruel owner to give the dog to her. A grandma also helps in *The Wreck of the Zanzibar* when Laura is trying to return the turtle to the sea before the gulls attack it or the islanders cut it up for turtle stew.

Granny May helps her feed the turtle with jellyfish and he swims back out to the ocean. Laura sees him being set free as a good omen. She imagines that the turtle will find her brother who has run way to sea and bring him safely home.

In *Why the Whales Came,* Gracie, Daniel and the birdman save another animal from becoming beached on the shore. This time it's a narwhale and by returning it to the sea they believe that they have saved the island from a terrible curse and returned Gracie's dad home safely from the First World War (Chapter 10, p. 119).

Often the children in Michael Morpurgo's stories have animals as their companions. They take the place of friends with animal and child becoming inseparable. Michael's dog Stella for a while becomes his only companion when he is washed up on an island in *Kensuke's Kingdom* (Chapter 4, p. 49). In *Dancing Bear* Roxanne adopts a bear cub (p. 11). However, unlike in *Butterfly Lion* and *War Horse* where child and animal are reunited when the child has become an adult, Bruno dies of a broken heart when Roxanne leaves the village where she was born, to pursue a career as a pop singer.

Relationships with grandparents and older people

While there are supportive parents in Michael Morpurgo's stories who have close relation-ships with their children (such as Laura's parents in *The Wreck of the Zanzibar,* Gracie's in *Why the Whales Came* and Cessie's in *Escape from Shangri-La*) there are many more examples of close relationships with older people. It is particularly their grandparents with whom the children feel most comfortable and can talk to because they understand each other so well. These are again echoes of Michael's own life as he did not know his father and was brought up in close contact with his grandparents.

The relationships between the children and the older generation are built on mutual trust and understanding. They make an effort to appreciate things from the other's point of view and realise that they each have knowledge that the other does not possess. Outsiders, and indeed the children's own parents, often only choose to see the idiosyncratic behaviour of the old people, forgetting the vast store of knowledge that they possess. They also often underestimate the children and what they feel and understand.

In *Why the Whales Came* Gracie and Daniel learn a lot from the birdman, Zachariah Woodcock, about nature and in particular birds, that are the old man's passion. The two children first have to overcome a fear of the old man that has been instilled in them by all the other islanders who let superstition and prejudice cloud their judgement (Chapter 2, p. 25). The culmination of their relationship comes when the three work together to save the narwhale.

However, relationships between the children and the older generation do not always go smoothly. When Michael is washed up on an island in the Pacific, he resents the actions of Kensuke (pronounced Kensky), a Japanese man who has been living on the island since he was shipwrecked there during the Second World War. At first the language barrier stops them communicating effectively and Michael misunderstands Kensuke's intentions when he tells Michael that he must not swim in the water. However, when a jellyfish stings Michael and Kensuke nurses him back to health, their relationship develops. Kensuke teaches Michael many skills necessary for surviving on the island and how to paint in the Japanese style on pottery. It is not until near the end of the story that they come to understand each other completely. Here they each recognise that the other is driven by different aims. Michael's is to be found and to return to his parents whereas Kensuke's is to protect the orang-utans that live on the island from poachers and to be allowed to live there quietly until he dies.

It is often the children's grandparents who help them out when they are in despair. It is Granny May who finds a way to get the turtle to go back into the sea in *The Wreck of the Zanzibar* (p. 69) and Grandma who goes with the vet to rescue the dog in *Conker*. Both these grandmas are full of commonsense advice, but they don't preach to the children. Instead they watch, suggest and listen and intervene when the time is right. Conversely, the children often help their grandparents. Cessie in *Escape From Shangri-La* helps her grandfather find himself again through his return trip to Dunkirk (Chapter 11, p. 150). These situations emphasise the strong bond that Morpurgo forms between these characters. An exception to this is the grandfather in *Dancing Bear*. He is portrayed as disinterested in the orphan Roxanne unless she provides him with a way to make money. The teacher, who narrates the story, fills the grandfather's place and, importantly, stands up for Roxanne against the grandfather when it seems that he will mistreat her

NLS reference to this type of work

By Year 3 pupils are expected to compare and contrast works by the same author which share similar themes. In Year 4 they look for evidence in the text for how characters deal with issues. Year 5 pupils are asked to write critically about theme and relate this to their understanding of the author's own experience. In Year 6 they are expected to explain and justify their preferences for authors, specifically in respect of theme.

Specific NLS Objectives

Y3: T2   To identify typical story themes.
Y4: T3   To identify moral, social or cultural issues in stories, e.g. the dilemmas faced by the characters or the moral of the story.
Y5: T1   To consider how text can be rooted in the writer's experience.
Y6: T1   To be familiar with the work of established authors, to know what is special about their work and to explain their preferences in terms of authors, styles and themes.

Activity: Book boxes

Comparing and contrasting works by Morpurgo is closely linked to finding out about the author. As many of his texts have their essence in his experiences and particular topics that are dear to him, the children will soon discover that there are particular themes that recur in his stories. (See the review of his work for information about these themes.) Focusing on the themes brings together information about the plots, characters and settings essential to a comparison of his books.

	Care of animals	Children who are solitary or isolated	Relationships between children and grandparents or older people	Farm and country life
Kensuke's Kingdom (LN)	✔	✔	✔	
Escape from Shangri-La (LN)		✔	✔	
Dancing Bear (SN)	✔	✔	✔	✔
Sam's Duck (PB)	✔		✔	✔
The Wreck of the Zanzibar (SN)	✔		✔	✔
Butterfly Lion (SN)	✔	✔	✔	
Why the Whales Came (LN)	✔		✔	✔
Farm Boy (SN)	✔		✔	✔
Conker (SS)	✔		✔	
Tom's Sausage Lion (SN)	✔	✔		✔
War Horse (LN)	✔			✔
Silver Swan (PB)	✔			✔
Rainbow Bear (PB)	✔			
Mudpuddle Farm titles in Jets series (SS)	✔			✔

Code: LN = longer novel; SN = shorter novel; SS = short story; PB = picture book

As you prepare to study a range of books by Morpurgo, put together a box or boxes of stories that you feel will go well together. Which stories you include will depend on the themes that you would like to explore and how you intend using the boxes with the children.

Organising group sessions with a book box

It is very important that the children have sufficient time to read the books and talk about them. This will enable the children to develop their perceptions and opinions and feed into writing activities in future lessons.

You will need to decide:

- Will the children read the stories individually or in pairs?
- Will the stories present a similar or different level of reading difficulty?
- Will you be part of the group discussion?
- Will you provide written open-ended prompts to aid discussion? (See question sheet).
- Will the group feedback orally the main points from their discussions to the rest of the class?
- Will the feedback to the class happen after all the groups have worked with a book box or straight after each group's session?

6 Comparing Stories – teaching sequence over five lessons

It is best if these lessons come towards the end of the author study, as they require the children to know quite a lot of information about a selection of stories. This series of lessons assumes that the book worked on in detail by each group is the one they began reading during the biographical work.

The whole classwork given for each lesson is followed by suggestions for group work asking the children to focus on one whole book or compare a small selection that they have read.

Whole class work

Lesson 1
Choose an extract from two books by Michael Morpurgo that the class is familiar with. Make sure that they either have similar characters, settings or storylines. Read these with the class and ask them to compare and contrast them. The prompts for group discussion (see sheet in the resources section) provide a good starting point for this session.

List the similarities and differences that the children suggest.

Lesson 2
Begin with the list of similarities from Lesson 1. Ask the children if any of the similarities that they thought of yesterday remind them of other characters, settings or storylines in books they have read by Michael Morpurgo. Develop their answers into a mind-map linking several stories by their characters, setting theme or plot.

Lesson 3
Introduce the children to the 'Who, What, Where' grid (p. 46). Fill in the titles of the books that you compared in Lesson 1. With the children, transfer the main similarities between the two books from the list onto the grid. Use this as an opportunity to look at how to summarise information and make notes about important points.

Lesson 4
Select an extract from a story that shows how Michael Morpurgo provides details about a main character. Show the children how you choose important words and phrases about the character from the passage. Do the words and phrases remind the children of any characters in other books?

Lesson 5

Ask the groups to feedback to the class where the stories that they have read are similar, by referring to examples from their grids. Ask the children to think what questions the stories raised for them and the questions that they thought Michael Morpurgo was trying to answer.

Group work

Teacher focus group

With the group discuss the storyline, setting and characters of the book they have read. Use the questions on the prompt sheet as a starting point. Ask the children to refer to the book to give particular examples from the text to illustrate their ideas and views. Can the children draw conclusions from explicit information given in the text (deduce)? Can they read between the lines and fill in the gaps that the author has left (infer)?

Responses from children discussing The Wreck of the Zanzibar with their teacher

What pictures do you have in your mind from reading *The Wreck of the Zanzibar*?
I can really see the beach, the cliffs, like where Laura found the turtle.

Are there similar places in any other books that you have read by Michael Morpurgo?
In Why the Whales Came – *that's on an island too.*

Does the beach in that book feel the same as in Zanzibar?
Yes. And in Why the Whales Came *something is washed up on that beach too – a whale.*

Independent activities

Many of these would work well with mixed ability groups; however, activities 2 and 4 are more suited to children who are independent learners.

1. In pairs the children compare two Michael Morpurgo titles that they have read. They list the similarities and differences between the two texts.

2. In pairs the children select a crucial event from a Morpurgo book that they have read. They then note the words and phrases that show how the characters are feeling or that create a picture of the setting. These could be shared with the class at the end of the lesson and form part of a display focusing on the way Morpurgo uses language. If the words and phrases are word-processed the children could categorise the phrases and experiment with fonts and layout to create a display for the wall.

3. In small groups the children complete the 'Who, What, Where' grid for their books, noting only the main points. They might like to use the prompts on p. 47.

4. In pairs or threes the children construct a story web showing the main events in one book. (See the example of a story web for *The Butterfly Lion* in the section on narrative structure p. 22.)

5. Ask the group to present the main points in the storyline of a Morpurgo story that they know well using three freeze-frames. Ask them to choose one freeze-frame to represent the opening, the climax and the resolution of the story.

6   In pairs the children develop a mind-map that shows the links they can see between a selection of Morpurgo's books.

Book Title	Who are the characters in the story?	What are the main points of the story line?	Where does the story take place?
Why the Whales came	Mother, Father, Daniel, Tim Gracie	Long Time ago 1914	Popplestone Bay Isles of Silly
The Wreck of the Zanzibar	Great - aunt house Uncle Bill, Michael Billy, house	Long Time ago 1907	In The Silly Isles
Farm Boy	Mother, Father Grandpa four Sisters great Grandfather grey	A Few years ago	On A Farm At Devon
Escape from Shangri-La	Mum, Mccrie and Grandad		At Home

PHOTOCOPIABLE SHEET

Book title	Who are the characters in the story?	What are the main points of the story-line?	Where does the story take place?

Prompts for group discussion

Setting

What pictures do you have in your mind from one story?

What feelings do you have about an important place in one story?

Which words or phrases helped you create that picture and give you those feelings?

Are there similar places in any other books that you have read by Michael Morpurgo?

How are similar places described in the books you've read? Do they sound or feel the same?

Story-line

What would you say this story is about?

What is the most important event in the story?

Are there any events in the books that you have read that are similar?

What is Morpurgo asking you to think about in these stories?

What are the important ideas in these books?

Characters

Is there anything similar about the characters in the books you've read?

Do any of the characters in different books have similar feelings?

Do any of the characters have similar problems to solve in the books you've read?

Are there any characters that act in the same way in different books?

Do boys and girls act differently in the books you've read?

Overall

What questions did you have as you read the books?

What questions do you think Morpurgo was trying to answer in these books?

7   In close: teaching sequence

Close study of one book – *The Butterfly Lion*

This magical story will entrance children throughout Key Stage 2. The ideas for working with this book would follow on well from looking at Michael Morpurgo as an author.

The approaches and activities arising from *The Butterfly Lion* are given in a suggested teaching order, following the chapters in the book, but without suggestions for specific timings. You will need to decide whether to do the activities with the whole class during shared reading and writing or whether they could be used for group work.

It is very important that the children have access to the whole text, not just extracts from it. This may involve reading the story aloud, using it as a group text and providing an audio tape.

Introduction

Read the Foreword to the story written by the author. Draw the children's attention to the sources of inspiration for the story that Morpurgo has listed. Discuss the difference between fact and fiction and highlight the factual sources that Morpurgo has used to create his fictional tale. Do the children realise that Morpurgo is talking to them as the readers of the book?

Chapters 1 and 2 – 'Chilblains and Semolina Pudding'

The story is written in the first person. In the opening chapter, the narrator sets the scene for the story. Ask the children what they find out about the narrator in this chapter. Do they think that the events he is going to tell us about happened recently? Can they give evidence from the text that support their views?

Make a list of the questions that the children have about the story once they have read the first chapter. Refer to these as you read the rest of the story. Are the questions answered directly in the text or can the children infer the answers from what they've heard or read?

Chapter 3 – 'Timbavati'

Hot-seat Bertie

Use the technique of hot-seating to allow the children to ask Bertie about his life in South Africa. This chapter provides a wealth of information about his life as a young boy. Decide whether you will take on the role of Bertie or whether a child or small group of children will collectively be Bertie. Whoever is assuming the role will need to become very familiar with the chapter entitled 'Timbavati' prior to being hot-seated by the class.

Before beginning the hot-seating session make sure that you have established a signal that lets the class know when the person or people are in role. This could be by wearing a particular article of clothing or sitting on a specific chair. During the hot-seating if 'Bertie' is unsure of the answer to a question then they can take off the clothing or stand up and declare themselves out of role as they are unsure of how to answer the question. This should not be seen as a negative experience, as a list can be made of unanswered questions and referred to when more of the story is known. If the questions are ones that you know the story will not answer then you could offer them to the class and ask for their opinions. This may provide an opportunity to draw their attention to the fact that as readers we may have different, but equally valid views about a story.

Character sketch of Bertie

Following the hot-seating the children can begin a character sketch of Bertie in shared writing. (See example of Laura Perryman from *Wreck of the Zanzibar'* on page 27 and the blank character sketch framework on page 28.) This will be added to at regular intervals during their reading of the story as they find out more about him.

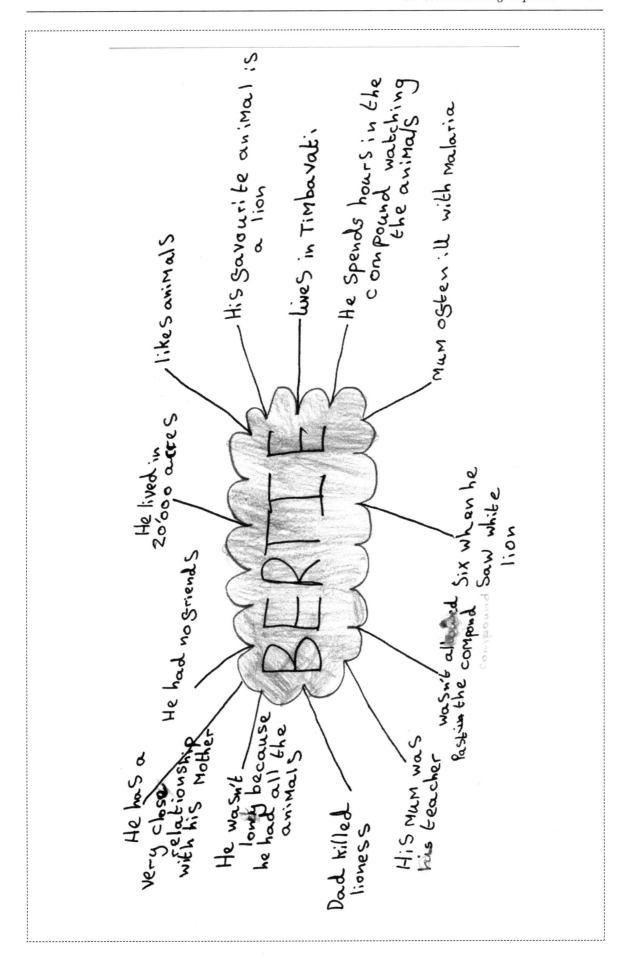

likes animals

His favourite animal is a lion

lives in Timbavati

He spends hours in the compound watching the animals

Mum often ill with malaria

He lived in 20'000 acres

BERTIE

He had no friends

He has a very close relationship with his mother

He wasn't lonly because he had all the animals

Dad killed lioness

His mum was his teacher

wasn't allowed past the compound

Six when he saw white lion

compound

My name is Bertie. I live in Timbavati in Africa. My mother is often ill with malaria. I'm not at all close with my father. He killed the white lioness! I was furious, but I was worried about the cub so I kept on looking out for him, but he never came. Not even once! Until one day I saw him. There were hyenas surrounding him! I ran out of my compound and saved him. My mother and I gave him a bath. Before that fateful day I had never, not even once, left my compound. I'm never lonely, believe it or not, and I love watching the wild animals that are free. I wish I was free, as free as the wind.

Susie

Find out about animals of the South African veld

This chapter introduces the children to the wildlife of the veld. Any of the activities below would enable them to become more familiar with the animals' habitat, food and way of life.

- Carry out research into lions using non-fiction books, CD-ROMs and the Internet. (See website suggestions on reverse of poster.) Use the information that they find out to create a poster, book, audio tape or multi-media guide to lions for the rest of the class or another class.

- List the other animals mentioned in the chapter and ask the children to choose one they would like to know more about. Display this information as suggested above.

Chapters 4, 5 and 6 – 'Bertie and the Lion', 'Running Free' and 'The Frenchman'

Exploring the thoughts of Bertie, mum and dad

These chapters focus on the changes that the lion cub brings to Bertie's life and that of his mother and father. Any or all of the following drama techniques (see p. 55 for glossary of terms) could be used to explore further how they all feel about the lion, and how mum and dad view the future. They could also act as a lead-in to writing in role as one of the characters.

- Create a forum theatre with three children representing Bertie, mother and father. Divide the rest of the class into three, with each third being one of the characters. Focus on either the scene where the lion has just arrived at the farm or where the father says he is going to be taken away. The three children representing the characters only say what the children in the three groups tell them to say. (This may be an opportunity to involve quiet children in speaking in front of an audience, as they will not have to think of what to say, only repeat what their group tells them.) If this is the first time the children have come across this technique, it would be good to demonstrate it by giving each character their first words yourself to start off the conversation.

- Create freeze-frames of key scenes from the chapters and ask the children to say what their character is thinking. (This is often called thought tracking.) If the child in the freeze-frame is not able to say what their characters thought, ask the rest of the class for suggestions.

- Create a thought tunnel with half the class being mum and half being dad. Place the children taking on the role of mum in a line opposite those being dad. Walk down the middle of the two lines and ask a child from each line in turn (i.e. mum, dad, mum, and so on) to give their thoughts about Bertie and the lion. Encourage the children to make their own comments, but also allow them to echo the views expressed by others as there is bound to be some similarity.

- Write thought bubbles for mum, dad and Bertie for specific moments in the story.

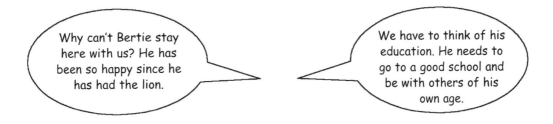

- Writing in role. Following on from the drama work the children could write in role as one of the characters, e.g. a letter from mother or father to Uncle George and Aunt Melanie, a diary entry by Bertie when he finds the lion and then a contrasting entry after his father has told him of his plans to sell his lion and send Bertie to school in England.

- Analyse how Bertie feels at the end of Chapter 6 ('The Frenchman'). Use the information given in the last paragraph in the chapter (p. 56 in Collins paperback) to begin a list of Bertie's positive and negative feelings.

Chapters 7, 8 and 9 – 'Strawbridge', 'And All's Well' and 'A lot of Old Codswallop'

- The children create their own character sketch of Millie or develop the one began as a class of Bertie.
- In pairs role-play part of Bertie and Millie's conversation on the afternoon they first meet. Some direct speech is given in Chapter 7 (pp. 62–7, Collins paperback), but there are two sections where Bertie tells Millie about his life in Africa and the white lion and where she tells Bertie about her life that are only referred to briefly. Ask the children to improvise one of these conversations using their knowledge of both characters and the plot so far.

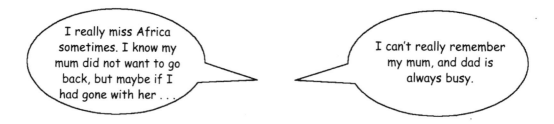

- The children write the above conversation either as a dialogue that could be inserted into Chapter 7 or as an extract from a playscript of the story.
- Chapters 8 and 9 provide much information about Bertie and Millie. This could be added to their character sketches.
- A role on the wall of Bertie could be completed for this part of the story. Draw an outline of Bertie on a large piece of paper. Inside the outline write how Bertie felt during his time in the First World War and outside comments on Bertie from the viewpoint of other characters.
- Write a newspaper report of the incident that gained Bertie the Victoria Cross.

Chapters 10 and 11 – 'The White Prince' and 'A Miracle, A Miracle!'

- Use forum theatre to work out how Bertie and Millie persuaded the colonel that the lion should stay at the hospital. The outline of the discussion on p. 109 (Collins paperback) provides a good starting point. Ask three children to take on the roles of Bertie, Millie and the colonel. The action is developed by using forum theatre, with the rest of the class making suggestions to the three characters about what they might say.
- Write a letter in role from Bertie to 'the powers that be in England' (p. 110, Collins paperback) to persuade them to let Bertie bring the lion back to England.

Chapters 12 and 13 – 'The Butterfly Lion, And the Lion Shall Lie Down With the Lamb' and 'Adonis Blues'

- List the many links in the last three chapters with earlier parts of the story.
- In pairs the children retell in role the events in the last two chapters. One child is Morpurgo and the other is a friend of his from the school who knows nothing about him running away from school. The friend can ask questions, and the child in role as Morpurgo can give their viewpoint on events.
- Write a diary entry in role as Morpurgo (this could be developed from the retelling above) giving the character's feelings and views based on events in the last two chapters.
- Create a temperature chart (sometimes known as an emotions map) of the last two chapters, illustrating Morpurgo's changing emotions. (See example of a temperature chart for *The Dancing Bear* in the section on narrative structure, p. 17.)

Glossary of drama terms

Freeze-frame: A frozen image of a moment in time, as if someone has taken a photograph.

Forum theatre: A small group of children act out a scene and are assisted by the rest of the class providing ideas for action and dialogue.

Thought tunnel: The class is divided into two groups to provide two points of view or two sides of a character's conscience.

Role on the wall: An outline drawing of a character is used as a focus for collating facts, feelings and views about the character.

Hot-seating: A teacher, pupil or group of pupils take on the role of a character so that the class (as themselves) can ask them questions.

Thought tracking: When the children are in role the children are asked what the character they are playing is thinking. This strategy works well with freeze-frames.

Wednesday 23rd Jan

The Synopsis of the
Butterfly Lion

1-2 Michael meets an old lady
in the street the old lady
tells him the story of th
Bertie and the White Lion.

3-5 3-8 (Africa)
Bertie meets the white
Lion cub.

6 The White Lion goes to the
circus in France the man is
called Monsieur Merlot.

7-8 Sadly his Mum says
"you have to go to England
to go to school.
He meets Millie.

9 when Bertie grows with
Millie they meet every Sunday to

fly their kites.

10-11 Bertie has grown up. He going to war.
The white Lion dies tray draw a chalky near a tree

12-14 Michael goes to school after
the lady has told the
story.
He finds Berties and the
White Lions grave, or

13 The old lady dies after
Michael has gone to school.
He knows it was not
a real person she was a ghost.
Michael will not forget the
Butterfly Lion or Bertie Andrews.